The Apocalypse of Peter

By Peter

Copyright © 2021 Lamp of Trismegistus. All rights reserved. No part of this publication may be reproduced or transmitted in any form or by any means, electronic or mechanical, including photocopying, recording, or by any information storage and retrieval system, without permission in writing from Lamp of Trismegistus. Reviewers may quote brief passages.

ISBN: 978-1-63118-527-4

Christian Apocrypha Series

Other Books in this Series and Related Titles

The Book of Wisdom of Solomon by King Solomon (978-1-63118-502-1)

The Gospel of the Nativity of Mary by St. Matthew (978-1-63118-448-2)

The Vision of Saint Paul the Apostle by Paul (978-1-63118-526-7)

Early Translation of the Acts of the Apostles by Luke (978-1-63118-521-2)

The Hymn of Jesus by G. R. S. Mead (978-1-63118-409-3)

Psalms of Solomon by King Solomon (978-1-63118-439-0)

The First and Second Gospels of the Infancy of Jesus Christ (978-1-63118-415-4)

The Book of Parables by Enoch (978-1-63118-429-1)

The Testament of Abraham by Abraham (978-1-63118-441-3)

The Lives of Adam and Eve by Moses (978-1-63118-414-7)

Masonic Symbolism of King Solomon's Temple by A Mackey &c (978-1-63118-442-0)

The Secrets of Enoch by Enoch (978-1-63118-449-9)

Lost Chapters of the Book of Daniel and Related Writings (978-1-63118-417-8)

The Testament of Moses by Moses (978-1-63118-440-6)

The Book of the Watchers by Enoch (978-1-63118-416-1)

Buddhist Psalms by Shinran (978-1-63118-465-9)

Masonic Symbolism of Easter and the Christ in Masonry (978-1-63118-434-5)

The Odes of Solomon by King Solomon (978-1-63118-503-8)

Book of Dreams by Enoch (978-1-63118-437-6)

The Hymns of Hermes by G. R. S. Mead (978-1-63118-405-5)

The Book of Astronomical Secrets by Enoch (978-1-63118-443-7)

Audio Versions are also Available on Audible, Amazon and Apple

Table of Contents

Series Introduction...7

Historical Notes to the Revelation or Apocalypse of Peter...9

The Apocalypse of Peter...17

Introduction by M. R. James...21

*Additional Translations of the Apocalypse of Peter
With Notes in Italics*

Section A: *Collected Quotations*...23

Section B: *The Akhmim Fragment*...26

The Bodleian Leaf...31

Section C: *The Ethiopic Text*...32

Appendix:
Second Book of the Sibylline Oracles, 190-338...49

SERIES INTRODUCTION

The Apocrypha are a loosely knit series of books, written by early vanguards of Christianity (covering the eras of both the old and new testaments), and which comprise somewhere between about a dozen to several hundred titles, depending on whom you ask and how that person defines "Apocrypha." A small selection of these can still be found included in the Catholic bible, while a majority of the books in question, were abandoned by church officials in the early centuries of Christianity. Many of these apocryphal books were originally considered canon by early followers of Christ, in the first four centuries following his birth. It wasn't until the meeting of the Council of Nicaea in 325, that Emperor Constantine and a group of roughly 300 church bishops, gathered together with the goal of defining, standardizing and unifying an otherwise splintering Christianity, that many of these writings ceased to be included in the newly established canon. Enjoy then, this book as an example, of just one of the many books of the Christian Apocrypha, and be sure to check out other titles in this series.

HISTORICAL NOTES TO THE REVELATION OR APOCALYPSE OF PETER

The fragment here translated was discovered in 1880 by the French Archaeological Mission in an ancient burying place at Akhmim in Upper Egypt. It was published at Paris in 1892 (*Bouriant, Mèmoires publiès par les membres de la Mission Archèologique Francaise au Caire*, T. ix., fasc. 1, 1892). The ms. is now in the Gizeh Museum and has been held to be of a date between the eighth and twelfth centuries. Until the discovery of the fragment, the following was all that was known about the Revelation of Peter.

1. The so-called *Muratorian Fragment*, a list of sacred writings, first published by Muratori in 1740, and found by him in a seventh or eighth century ms. belonging to the Ambrosian Library in Milan, but which had previously belonged to the Columban Monastery of Bobbio, is assigned on internal evidence to the third quarter of the second century. (*Vide* Westcott, *Canon of the* N. T., p. 514.) At line 60 it says: "the Apocalypses also of John and Peter only do we receive, which (latter) some among us would not have read in church."

2. Clement of Alexandria (fl. c. 200 a.d.) in his *Hypotoposes*, according to the testimony of Eusebius, *H. E.*, vi., 14, gave "abridged accounts of all the canonical Scriptures, not even omitting those that are disputed, I mean the book of Jude and the other general epistles. Also the Epistle of Barnabas and that called the Revelation of Peter." Also in his *Eclogoe Propheticae*, chapters 41, 48 and 49, he gives three, or as some think, four quotations from the Revelation of Peter, mentioning it twice by name.

3. The *Catalogue Claromontanus*, an Eastern list of Holy Scriptures, belonging to the third century, gives at the end the Revelation of Peter (v. Westcott, *Canon*, p. 55). This catalogue gives the length of the various books it enumerates measured in stichoi. Our book is said to have two hundred and seventy, which makes it rather longer than the Epistle to the Colossians which has two hundred and fifty-one.

4. Methodius, bishop of Olympus in Lycia in the beginning of the fourth century, in his *Symposium*, ii., 6, says, "wherefore we have also learned from divinely inspired Scriptures that untimely births even if they are the offspring of adultery are delivered to caretaking angels." Though Peter is not here mentioned, the purport of the passage is the same as that of one of the quotations given by Clement of Alexandria.

5. Eusebius (_ *c.* 339 a.d.), in his *Ecclesiastical History*, iii., 25, expressly mentions the Revelation of Peter along with the Acts of Paul and the *Pastor* as spurious books, while at iii., 3, he says: "as to that which is called the *Preaching* and that called the Apocalypse of Peter, we know nothing of their being handed down as Catholic writings. Since neither among the ancients nor among the ecclesiastical writers of our own day, has there been anyone that has appealed to testimony taken from them."

6. Macarius Magnes (beginning of fifth century) in his *Apocritica,*, iv., 6 quotes as from a heathen opponent of Christianity the following: "Let us by way of superfluity cite also that saying in the Apocalypse of Peter. It thus introduces the heaven as being about to undergo judgment along with the earth. `The earth, 'it says, `shall present all men before God at the day of judgment, being itself also to be judged along with the heaven also which

encompasses it.'" And at iv., 16, he examines this passage again, naming the revelation of Peter, and supporting the doctrine of the passage by the authority of prophecy (Isaiah 34:4) and the Gospel (Matthew 24:85).

7. Sozomen (middle of fifth century), *H. E.*, vii., 19, says: "For instance, the so-called Apocalypse of Peter which was esteemed as entirely spurious by the ancients, we have discovered to be read in certain churches of Palestine up to the present day, once a, year, on the day of preparation, during which the people most religiously fast in commemoration of the Saviour's Passion" (i.e., on Good Friday). It is to be noted that Sozomen himself belonged to Palestine.

8. In the list of *the Sixty Books* which is assigned to the fifth or sixth century the Revelation of Peter is mentioned among the Apocrypha (v. Westcott, *Canon*, p. 551).

9. The so-called *Stichometry of Nicephorus*, a list of scriptures with notes of their extent, ascribed to Nicephorus, Patriarch of Constantinople, 806-814 a.d., includes the Revelation of Peter among the *antilegomena* or disputed writings of the New Testament, and gives it three hundred stichoi or thirty more than the above-mentioned Catalogus Claromontanas.

10. The Armenian annalist Mkhitan (thirteenth century) in a list of the New Testament antilegomena mentions the Revelation of Peter, after the Gospel of Thomas and before the *Periodoi Pauli*, and remarks that he has himself copied these books. (Cf. Harnack, *Geschichte der altchristlichen Literatur.*)

Up till lately these facts represented all that was positively known of the Revelation of Peter. From them we gather that it must have been written before the middle of the second. century (so as to be known at Rome and included in the Muratorian Canon), that it had a wide circulation, that it was for some time very popular, so that it would appear to have run a considerable chance of achieving a place in the canon, but that it was ultimately rejected and in the long run dropped out of knowledge altogether. But even previously to the discovery at Akhméɶm, the general character of the book had been inferred from the scanty fragments preserved in ancient writers and from the common elements contained in other and later apocalyptic writings which seemed to require some such book as the Revelation of Peter as their ultimate source. Such writings are the (Christian) Apocalypse of Esdras, the Vision of Paul, the Passion of S. Perpetua and the visions contained in the History of Barlaam and Josaphat. (Cf. Robinson, *Texts and Studies*, i., 2, p. 37-43, and Robinson and James, *The Gospel according to Peter and the Revelation of Peter*, 1892.)

The Revelation of Peter affords the earliest embodiment in Christian literature of those pictorial presentations of heaven and hell which have exercised so widespread and enduring an influence. It has, in its imagery, little or no kinship with the Book of Daniel, the Book of Enoch, or the Revelation of S. John. Its only parallels in canonical scripture, with the notable exception of the Second Epistle of Peter, are to be found in Isaiah lxvi., 24, Mark ix., 44, 48, and the parable of Dives and Lazarus in Luke xvi., 19. It is indeed Judaic in the severity of its morality and even in its phraseology (*cf.* the frequent use of the word *righteous*, and the idea that God and not Christ will come to judge sinners). Rut the true parallels for, if not the sources of, its imagery of the rewards and punishments which await men after death are to be found in Greek beliefs which have left their traces in such passages as the Vision of Er at the end of Plato's *Republic*.

The heaven of the Petrine Apocalypse is akin to the Elysian Fields and the Islands of the Blest. In it the saints are crowned as with flowers and beautiful of countenance, singing songs of praise in the fragrant air, in a land all lighted up with the light of the sun.[1] We are reminded of "the Elysian Fields and the world's end where is Rhadamanthus of the fair hair, where life is easiest for men. No snow is there, nor yet great storm, nor any rain; but alway Ocean sendeth forth the breeze of the shrill West to blow cool on men" (*Odyssey*, iv., 568), and of the garden of the gods on Olympus, which "is not shaken by winds, or ever wet with rain, nor doth the snow come nigh thereto, but most clear air is spread about it cloudless, and the white light floats over it" (*Odyssey*, vi., 43, Butcher and Lang's transl.). Perhaps the most striking parallel of all is afforded by the fragment of a dirge of Pindar: "For them shineth below the strength of the sun, while in our world it is night, and the space of crimson-flowered meadow before their city is full of the shade of frankincense trees, and of fruits of gold. And some in horses, and in bodily feats, and some in dice, and some in harp-playing have delight; and among them thriveth all fair-flowering bliss; and fragrance streameth ever through the lovely land, as they mingle incense of every kind upon the altars of the gods" (Pindar, E. Myer's transl., p. 116). Beside this heaven the New Jerusalem of the canonical Apocalypse is austere. But it is the spiritual city. "For the city had no need of the sun, neither of the moon to shine on it, for the Lord God Almighty and the Lamb were in the midst of it and the Lamb was the light thereof."

So likewise in the case of the torments of the wicked as presented in the Revelation of Peter. We are not here in the Jewish Sheol, or among the fires of the valley of Hinnom, so much as among the tortures of Tartarus and the boiling mud of the Acherusian Lake (*cf.* Plato, *Phaedo*, p. 113; Aristophanes, *Frogs*, line

145), or where "wild men of fiery aspect... seized and. carried off several of them, and Ardiaeus and others, they bound head and foot and hand, and threw them down and flayed them with scourges, and dragged them along the road at the side, carding them on thorns like wool, and declaring to the passers-by what were their crimes, and that they were being taken away to be cast into hell" (*Republic*, x., p. 616, Jowett's transl.). It is not surprising that in later visions of the same kind the very names of the Greek under-world are ascribed to localities of hell. It is across the river Oceanus. It is called Tartarus, In it is the Acherusian Lake. Notice in this connection that the souls of innocent victims are present along with their murderers to accuse them.

The Revelation of Peter shows remarkable kinship in ideas with the Second Epistle of Peter. The parallels will be noted in the margin of the translation. It also presents notable parallels to the Sibylline Oracles (*cf. Orac. Sib.*, ii., 225 sqq.), while its influence has been conjectured, almost with certainty, in the Acts of Perpetua and. the visions narrated in the Acts of Thomas and the History of Barlaam and Josaphat. It certainly was one of the sources from which the writer of the Vision of Paul drew. And directly or indirectly it may be regarded as the parent of all the mediaeval visions of the other world.

The fragment begins in the middle of an eschatological discourse of Jesus, probably represented as delivered after the resurrection, for verse 5 implies that the disciples had begun to preach the Gospel. It ends abruptly in the course of a catalogue of sinners in hell and their punishments. The fragments preserved in the writings of Clement of Alexandria and Methodius probably belonged to the lost end of the book; that preserved by Macarius Magnes may have belonged to the eschatological discourse at the beginning. Taking the length of the whole at from two hundred and seventy to three hundred stichoi, the Akhmim fragment contains about the half.

The present translation is made from Harnack's edition of the text, 2d ed., Leipzig, 1893.

There is another and later Apocalypse of Peter in Arabic, of which mss. exist in Rome and Oxford. It is called the Apocalypse of Peter, or the narrative of things revealed to him by Jesus Christ which had taken place from the beginning of the world and which shall take place till the end of the world or the second coming of Christ. The book is said to have been written by Clement, to whom Peter had communicated the secrets revealed to him. The writer himself calls the book *Librum Perfectionis* or *Librum Completum*. Judging from the analysis of its contents quoted by Tischendorf (Apocalypses Apocr.) it has no connection with the present work.

THE APOCALYPSE OF PETER

1. ... many of them will be false prophets, and will teach divers ways and doctrines of perdition: but these will become sons of perdition.

3. And then God will come unto my faithful ones who hunger and thirst and are afflicted and purify their souls in this life; and he will judge the sons of lawlessness.

4. And furthermore the Lord said: Let us go into the mountain: Let us pray.

5. And going with him, we, the twelve disciples, begged that he would show us one of our brethren, the righteous who are gone forth out of the world, in order that we might see of what manner of form they are, and having taken courage, might also encourage the men who hear us.

6. And as we prayed, suddenly there appeared two men standing before the Lord towards the East, on whom we were not able to look;

7, for there came forth from their countenance a ray as of the sun, and their raiment was shining, such as eye of man never saw; for no mouth is able to express or heart to conceive the glory with which they were endued, and the beauty of their appearance.

8. And as we looked upon them, we were astounded; for their bodies were whiter than any snow and ruddier than any rose;

9, and the red thereof was mingled with the white, and I am utterly unable to express their beauty;

10, for their hair was curly and bright and seemly both on their face and shoulders, as it were a wreath woven of spikenard and divers-coloured flowers, or like a rainbow in the sky, such was their seemliness.

11. Seeing therefore their beauty we became astounded at them, since they appeared suddenly.

12. And I approached the Lord and said: Who are these?

13. He saith to me: These are your brethren the righteous, whose forms ye desired to see.

14. And I said to him: And where are all the righteous ones and what is the aeon in which they are and have this glory?

15. And the Lord showed me a very great country outside of this world, exceeding bright with light, and the air there lighted with the rays of the sun, and the earth itself blooming with unfading flowers and full of spices and plants, fair-flowering and incorruptible and bearing blessed fruit.

16. And so great was the perfume that it was borne thence even unto us.

17. And the dwellers in that place were clad in the raiment of shining angels and their raiment was like unto their country; and angels hovered about them there.

18. And the glory of the dwellers there was equal, and with one voice they sang praises alternately to the Lord God, rejoicing in that place.

19. The Lord saith to us: This is the place of your high-priests, the righteous men.

20. And over against that place I saw another, squalid, and it was the place of punishment; and those who were punished there and the punishing angels had their raiment dark like the air of the place.

21. And there were certain there hanging by the tongue: and these were the blasphemers of the way of righteousness; and under them lay fire, burning and punishing them.

22. And there was a great lake, full of flaming mire, in which were certain men that pervert righteousness, and tormenting angels afflicted them.

23. And there were also others, women, hanged by their hair over that mire that bubbled up: and these were they who adorned

themselves for adultery; and the men who mingled with them in the defilement of adultery, were hanging by the feet and their heads in that mire. *And* I said: I did not believe that I should come into this place.

24. And I saw the murderers and those who conspired with them, cast into a certain strait place, full of evil snakes, and smitten by those beasts, and thus turning to and fro in that punishment; and worms, as it were clouds of darkness, afflicted them. And the souls of the murdered stood and looked upon the punishment of those murderers and said: O God, thy judgment is just.

25. And near that place I saw another strait place into which the gore and the filth of those who were being punished ran down and became there as it were a lake: and there sat women having the gore up to their necks, and over against them sat many children who were born to them out of due time, crying; and there came forth from them sparks of fire and smote the women in the eyes: and these were the accursed who conceived and caused abortion.

26. And other men and women were burning up to the middle and were cast into a dark place and were beaten by evil spirits, and their inwards were eaten by restless worms: and these were they who persecuted the righteous and delivered them up.

27. And near those there were again women and men gnawing their own lips, and being punished and receiving a red-hot iron in their eyes: and these were they who blasphemed and slandered the way of righteousness.

28. And over against these again other men and women gnawing their tongues and having flaming fire in their mouths: and these were the false witnesses.

29. And in a certain other place there were pebbles sharper than swords or any spit, red-hot, and women and men in tattered and filthy raiment rolled about on them in punishment: and these were

the rich who trusted in their riches and had no pity for orphans and widows, and despised the commandment of God.

30. And in another great lake, full of pitch and blood and mire bubbling up, there stood men and women up to their knees: and these were the usurers and those who take interest on interest.

31. And other men and women were being hurled down from a great cliff and reached the bottom, and again were driven by those who were set over them to climb up upon the cliff, and thence were hurled down again, and had no rest from this punishment: and these were they who defiled their bodies acting as women; and the women who were with them were those who lay with one another as a man with a woman.

32. And alongside of that cliff there was a place full of much fire, and there stood men who with their own hands had made for themselves carven images instead of God. And alongside of these were other men and women, having rods and striking each other and never ceasing from such punishment.

33. And others again near them, women and men, burning and turning themselves and roasting: and these were they that leaving the way of God

INTRODUCTION BY M. R. JAMES

We have not a pure and complete text of this book, which ranked next in popularity and probably also in date to the Canonical Apocalypse of St. John.

We have, first (*section A*), certain quotations made by writers of the first four centuries.

Next (*section B*), a fragment in Greek, called the Akhmim fragment, found with the Passion-fragment of the Gospel of Peter in a manuscript known as the Gizeh MS. (discovered in a tomb) now at Cairo. This is undoubtedly drawn from the Apocalypse of Peter: but my present belief is that, like the Passion fragment (see p. 90), it is part of the Gospel of Peter, which was a slightly later book than the Apocalypse and quoted it almost in extenso. There is also in the Bodleian Library a mutilated leaf of a very tiny Greek MS. of the fifth century which supplies a few lines of what I take to be the original Greek text.

Thirdly (*section C*), an Ethiopic version contained in one of the numerous forms of the books of Clement, a writing current in Arabic and Ethiopic purporting to contain revelations of the history of the world from the Creation, of the last times, and of guidance for the churches -dictated by Peter to Clement. The version of the Apocalypse contained in this has some extraneous matter at the beginning and the end; but, as I have tried to show in a series of articles in the *Journal of Theological Studies* (1910-11) and the Church Quarterly Review (1915), it affords the best general idea of the contents of the whole book which we have. The second book of the Sibylline Oracles contains (in Greek hexameters) a paraphrase of a great part of the Apocalypse: and its influence can be traced in many early writings -the Acts of Thomas (55-57), the Martyrdom of Perpetua, the so-called Second Epistle of Clement, and, as I think, the Shepherd of Hermas: as well as in the Apocalypse of Paul and many later visions.

The length of the book is given in the Stichometry of Nicephorus as 300 lines and in that of the Codex Claromontanus (D of the Epistle) as 270: the latter is a Latin list of the Biblical books; already cited for the Acts of Paul.

There is no mention of it in the Gelasian Decree, which is curious. At one time it was popular in Rome for the Muratorian Canon mentions it (late in the second century?) along with the Apocalypse of John though it adds, that 'some will not have it read in the church.' The fifth-century church historian Sozomen (vii. 19) says that to his knowledge it was still read annually in some churches in Palestine on Good Friday.

A translation of the ancient quotations shall be given first.

ADDITIONAL TRANSLATIONS

TEXTS OF THE APOCALYPSE OF PETER
With Notes in Italics

A.

1. *From Clement of Alexandria's so-called Prophetical Extracts, a series of detached sentences excerpted from some larger work, generally supposed to be his Hypotyposes or Outlines:*

a. (41.1) The Scripture saith that the children which have been exposed (by their parents) are delivered to a care-taking angel by whom they are educated, and made to grow up, and they shall be, it saith, as the faithful of an hundred years old are here (in this life). b. (41.2) Wherefore also Peter in the Apocalypse saith: And a flash (lightning) of fire leaping from those children and smiting the eyes of the women.

2. *Ibid. (48.1)* The providence of God doth not light upon them only that are in the flesh. For example, Peter in the Apocalypse saith that the children born out of due time (abortively) that would have been of the better part (i. e. would have been saved if they had lived) -these are delivered to a care-taking angel, that they may partake of knowledge and obtain the better abode, having suffered what they would have suffered had they been in the body. But the others (i.e. those who would not have been saved, had they lived) shall only obtain salvation, as beings that have been injured and had mercy shown to them, and shall continue without torment, receiving that as a reward.

But the milk of the mothers, flowing from their breasts and congealing, saith Peter in the Apocalypse, shall engender small beasts (snakes) devouring the flesh, and these running upon them devour them: teaching that the torments come to pass because of the sins (correspond to the sins).

3. *From the Symposium (ii.6) of Methodius of Olympus (third century). He does not name his source.* Whence also we have received in inspired writings that children born untimely -even if they be the offspring of adultery- are delivered to care-taking angels. For if they had come into being contrary to the will and ordinance of that blessed nature of God, how could they have been delivered to angels to be nourished up in all repose and tranquillity? And how could they have confidently summoned their parents before the judgement seat of Christ to accuse them? saying: Thou, O Lord, didst not begrudge us this light that is common to all, but these exposed us to death, contemning thy commandment.

The word rendered care-taking in these passages is a very rare one- [temelouchos, Gr.]: so rare that it was mistaken by later readers for the proper name of an angel, and we find an angel Temeluchus in Paul, John, and elsewhere. A similar case is that of the word Tartaruchus, keeper of hell, which is applied to angels in our Apocalypse, and is also taken in the Ethiopic version, in Paul, and in other writings, to be a proper name.

4. *From the Apocritica of Macarius Magnes (fourth century) of whom we know little. His book consists of extracts from a heathen opponent's attack on Christianity (Porphyry and Hieroclcs are named as possible authors of it) and his own answers. The heathen writer says (iv. 6, 7):*

And by way of superfluity let this also be cited which is said in the Apocalypse of Peter. He introduces the Heaven, to be judged along with the earth, thus: The earth, he says, shall present all men to God to be judged in the day of judgement being itself also to be judged along with the heaven that encompasseth it.

5. *Ibid.* And this again he says, which is a statement full of impiety: And every power of heaven shall be melted, and the heaven shall be rolled up like a book, and all the stars shall fall like leaves from the vine, and as the leaves from the fig-tree.

This very nearly coincides with Isa. xxxiv.4, and does not occur in our other texts of the Apocalypse.

6. In an old Latin homily on the Ten Virgins found and published by Dom Wilmart (Bulletin d'anc. litt. et d'arche'ol. chre't.) is this sentence:

The closed door is the river of fire by which the ungodly shall be kept out of the kingdom of God, as is written in Daniel and in Peter, in his Apocalypse.... That company of the foolish also shall arise and find the door shut, that is, the fiery river set against them.

The equivalent of all the above quotations is found in the Ethiopic text, with one exception, no. 5. The Akhmim text only contains Something like no. 1 b: one indication out of many that it is a shortened and, I would say, secondary text.

B.

THE AKHMIM FRAGMENT

I should prefer to call this Fragment II of the Gospel of Peter. It begins abruptly in a discourse of our Lord.

1 Many of them shall be false prophets, and shall teach ways and diverse doctrines of perdition.

2 And they shall become sons of perdition.

3 And then shall God come unto my faithful ones that hunger and thirst and are afflicted and prove their souls in this life, and shall judge the sons of iniquity.

4 And the Lord added and said: Let us go unto the mountain (and) pray.

5 And going with him, we the twelve disciples besought him that he would show us one of our righteous brethren that had departed out of the world, that we might see what manner of men they are in their form, and take courage, and encourage also the men that should hear us.

6 And as we prayed, suddenly there appeared two men standing before the Lord (perhaps add, to the east) upon whom we were not able to look.

7 For there issued from their countenance a ray as of the sun, and their raiment was shining so as the eye of man never saw the

like: for no mouth is able to declare nor heart to conceive the glory wherewith they were clad and the beauty of their countenance.

8 Whom when we saw we were astonied, for their bodies were whiter than any snow and redder than any rose.

9 And the redness of them was mingled with the whiteness, and, in a word, I am not able to declare their beauty.

10 For their hair was curling and flourishing (flowery), and fell comely about their countenance and their shoulders like a garland woven of nard and various flowers, or like a rainbow in the air: such was their comeliness.

11 We, then, seeing the beauty of them were astonied at them, for they appeared suddenly.

12 And I drew near to the Lord and said: Who are these?

13 He saith to me: These are your (our) righteous brethren whose appearance ye did desire to see.

14 And I said unto him: And where are all the righteous? or of what sort is the world wherein they are, and possess this glory?

15 And the Lord showed me a very great region outside this world exceeding bright with light, and the air of that place illuminated with the beams of the sun, and the earth of itself flowering with blossoms that fade not, and full of spices and plants, fair-flowering and incorruptible, and bearing blessed fruit.

16 And so great was the blossom that the odour thereof was borne thence even unto us.

17 And the dwellers in that place were clad with the raiment of shining angels, and their raiment was like unto their land.

18 And angels ran round about them there.

19 And the glory of them that dwelt there was all equal, and with one voice they praised the Lord God, rejoicing in that place.

20 The Lord saith unto us: This is the place of your leaders (or, high priests), the righteous men.

21 And I saw also another place over against that one, very squalid; and it was a place of punishment, and they that were punished and the angels that punished them had their raiment dark, according to the air of the place.

22 And some there were there hanging by their tongues; and these were they that blasphemed the way of righteousness, and under them was laid fire flaming and tormenting them.

23 And there was a great lake full of flaming mire, wherein were certain men that turned away from righteousness; and angels, tormentors, were set over them.

24 And there were also others, women, hanged by their hair above that mire which boiled up; and these were they that adorned themselves for adultery.

And the men that were joined with them in the defilement of adultery were hanging by their feet, and had their heads hidden in the mire, and said: We believed not that we should come unto this place.

25 And I saw the murderers and them that were consenting to them cast into a strait place full of evil, creeping things, and smitten by those beasts, and so turning themselves about in that torment. And upon them were set worms like clouds of darkness. And the souls of them that were murdered stood and looked upon the torment of those murderers and said: O God, righteous is thy judgement.

26 And hard by that place I saw another strait place wherein the discharge and the stench of them that were in torment ran down, and there was as it were a lake there. And there sat women up to their necks in that liquor, and over against them many children which were born out of due time sat crying: and from them went forth rays of fire and smote the women in the eyes: and these were they that conceived out of wedlock (?) and caused abortion.

27 And other men and women were being burned up to their middle and cast down in a dark place and scourged by evil spirits, and having their entrails devoured by worms that rested not. And these were they that had persecuted the righteous and delivered them up.

28 And near to them again were women and men gnawing their lips and in torment, and having iron heated in the fire set against their eyes. And these were they that did blaspheme and speak evil of the way of righteousness.

29 And over against these were yet others, men and women, gnawing their tongues and having flaming fire in their mouths. And these were the false witnesses.

30 And in another place were gravel-stones sharper than swords or any spit, heated with fire, and men and women clad in filthy rags rolled upon them in torment. [This is suggested by the LXX of two passages in Job: xli. 30, his bed is of sharp spits; viii. 17, on an heap of stones doth he rest, and shall live in the midst of gravel-stones.] And these were they that were rich and trusted in their riches, and had no pity upon orphans and widows but neglected the commandments of God.

31 And in another great lake full of foul matter (pus) and blood and boiling mire stood men and women up to their knees And these were they that lent money and demanded usury upon usury.

32 And other men and women being cast down from a great rock (precipice) fell (came) to the bottom, and again were driven by them that were set over them, to go up upon the rock, and thence were cast down to the bottom and had no rest from this torment. And these were they that did defile their bodies behaving as women: and the women that were with them were they that lay with one another as a man with a woman.

33 And beside that rock was a place full of much fire, and there stood men which with their own hands had made images for themselves instead of God, [And beside them other men and women] having rods of fire and smiting one another and never resting from this manner of torment....

34 And yet others near unto them, men and women, burning and turning themselves about and roasted as in a pan. And these were they that forsook the way of God.

THE BODLEIAN LEAF

It measures but 2 3/4 by 2 inches and has 13 lines of 8 to 10 letters on each side (Madan's Summary Catalogue, No. 31810). The verso (second page) is difficult to read.

Recto=Gr. 33, 34: women holding chains and scourging themselves before those idols of deceit. And they shall unceasingly have this torment. And near

Verso: them shall be other men and women burning in the burning of them that were mad after idols. And these are they which forsook the way of God wholly (?) and . . .

C.

THE ETHIOPIC TEXT

First published by the Abbe Sylvain Grebaut in Revue de l'Orient Chretien, 1910: a fresh translation from his Ethiopic text by H. Duensing appeared in Zeitschr. f. ntl. Wiss., 1913.

The Second Coming of Christ and Resurrection of the Dead (which Christ revealed unto Peter) who died because of their sins, for that they kept not the commandment of God their creator.

And he (Peter) pondered thereon, that he might perceive the mystery of the Son of God, the merciful and lover of mercy.

And when the Lord was seated upon the Mount of Olives, his disciples came unto him.

And we besought and entreated him severally and prayed him, saying unto him: Declare unto us what are the signs of thy coming and of the end of the world, that we may perceive and mark the time of thy coming and instruct them that come after us, unto whom we preach the word of thy gospel, and whom we set over (in) thy church, that they when they hear it may take heed to themselves and mark the time of thy coming.

And our Lord answered us, saying: Take heed that no man deceive you, and that ye be not doubters and serve other gods. Many shall come in my name, saying: I am the Christ. Believe them not, neither draw near unto them. For the coming of the Son of God shall not be plain (i.e. foreseen); but as the lightning that shineth from the east unto the west, so will I come upon the clouds of heaven with a great host in my majesty; with my cross going before my face will I come in my majesty, shining sevenfold more than the sun will I come in my majesty with all my saints, mine angels (mine holy angels). And my Father shall set a crown upon mine head, that I may judge the quick and the dead and recompense every man according to his works.

And ye, take ye the likeness thereof (learn a parable) from the fig-tree: so soon as the shoot thereof is come forth and the twigs grown, the end of the world shall come.

And I, Peter, answered and said unto him: Interpret unto me concerning the fig-tree, whereby we shall perceive it; for throughout all its days doth the fig-tree send forth shoots, and every year it bringeth forth its fruit for its master. What then meaneth the parable of the fig-tree? We know it not.

And the Master (Lord) answered and said unto me: Understandest thou not that the fig-tree is the house of Israel? Even as a man that planted a fig-tree in his garden, and it brought forth no fruit. And he sought the fruit thereof many years and when he found it not, he said to the keeper of his garden: Root up this fig-tree that it make not our ground to be unfruitful. And the gardener said unto God: (Suffer us) to rid it of weeds and dig the ground round about it and water it. If then it bear not fruit, we will straightway remove its roots out of the garden and plant another in place of it. Hast thou not undErstood that the fig-tree is the house of Israel? Verily I say unto thee, when the twigs thereof have sprouted forth in the last days, then shall feigned Christs come and awake expectation saying: I am the Christ, that am now come into the world. And when they (Israel) shall perceive the wickedness of their deeds they shall turn away after them and deny him [whom our fathers did praise], even the first Christ whom they crucified and therein sinned a great sin. But this deceiver is not the Christ. [something is wrong here: the sense required is that Israel perceives the wickedness of antichrist and does not follow him.] And when they reject him he shall slay with the sword, and there shall be many martyrs. Then shall the twigs of the fig-tree, that is, the house of Israel, shoot forth: many shall become martyrs at his hand. Enoch and Elias shall be sent to teach them that this is the deceiver which must come into the world and do signs and wonders to deceive. And therefore shall they that die by his hand be martyrs, and shall be reckoned among the good and righteous martyrs who have pleased God in their life. [Hermas, Vision III.i.9, speaks of 'those that have already been well-pleasing unto God and have suffered for the Name's sake'.]

And he showed me in his right hand the souls of all men, And on the palm of his right hand the image of that which shall be accomplished at the last day: and how the righteous and the sinners shall be separated, and how they do that are upright in heart, and how the evil-doers shall be rooted out unto all eternity. We beheld how the sinners wept (weep) in great affliction and sorrow, until all that saw it with their eyes wept, whether righteous or angels, and he himself also.

And I asked him and said unto him: Lord, suffer me to speak thy word concerning the sinners: It were better for them if they had not been created. And the Saviour answered and said unto me: Peter, wherefore speakest thou thus, that not to have been created were better for them? Thou resistest God. Thou wouldest not have more compassion than he for his image: for he hath created them and brought them forth out of not being. Now because thou hast seen the lamentation which shall come upon the sinners in the last days, therefore is thine heart troubled; but I will show thee their works, whereby they have sinned against the Most High.

Behold now what shall come upon them in the last days, when the day of God and the day of the decision of the judgement of God cometh. From the east unto the west shall all the children of men be gathered together before my Father that liveth forever. And he shall command hell to open its bars of adamant and give up all that is therein.

And the wild beasts and the fowls shall he command to restore all the flesh that they have devoured, because he willeth that men should appear; for nothing perisheth before God, and nothing is impossible with him, because all things are his.

For all things come to pass on the day of decision, on the day of judgement, at the word of God: and as all things were done when he created the world and commanded all that is therein and it was done -even so shall it be in the last days; for all things are possible with God. And therefore saith he in the scripture: [Ezek. xxxvii.] Son of man, prophesy upon the several bones and say unto the bones: bone unto bone in joints, sinew. nerves, flesh and skin and hair thereon [and soul and spirit].

And soul and spirit shall the great Uriel give them at the commandment of God; for him hath God set over the rising again of the dead at the day of judgement.

Behold and consider the corns of wheat that are sown in the earth. As things dry and without soul do men sow them in the earth: and they live again and bear fruit, and the earth restoreth them as a pledge entrusted unto it.

[And this that dieth, that is sown as seed in the earth, and shall become alive and be restored unto life, is man. Probably a gloss.]

How much more shall God raise up on the day of decision them that believe in him and are chosen of him, for whose sake he made the world? And all things shall the earth restore on the day of decision, for it also shall be judged with them, and the heaven with it.

And this shall come at the day of judgement upon them that have fallen away from faith in God and that have committed sin: Floods (cataracts) of fire shall be let loose; and darkness and obscurity shall come up and clothe and veil the whole world and the waters shall be changed and turned into coals of fire and all that is in them shall burn, and the sea shall become fire. Under the heaven shall be a sharp fire that cannot be quenched and floweth to fulfil the judgement of wrath. And the stars shall fly in pieces by flames of fire, as if they had not been created and the powers (firmaments) of the heaven shall pass away for lack of water and shall be as though they had not been. And the lightnings of heaven shall be no more, and by their enchantment they shall affright the world (probably: The heaven shall turn to lightning and the lightnings thereof shall affright the world. The spirits also of the dead bodies shall be like unto them (the lightnings?) and shall become fire at the commandment of God.

And so soon as the whole creation dissolveth, the men that are in the east shall flee unto the west, unto the east; they that are in the south shall flee to the north, and they that are in the south. And in all places shall the wrath of a fearful fire overtake them and an unquenchable flame driving them shall bring them unto the judgement of wrath, unto the stream of unquenchable fire that floweth, flaming with fire, and when the waves thereof part themselves one from another, burning, there shall be a great gnashing of teeth among the children of men.

Then shall they all behold me coming upon an eternal cloud of brightness: and the angels of God that are with me shall sit (prob. And I shall sit) upon the throne of my glory at the right hand of my Heavenly Father; and he shall set a crown upon mine head. And when the nations behold it, they shall weep, every nation apart.

Then shall he command them to enter into the river of fire while the works of every one of them shall stand before them (something is wanting) to every man according to his deeds. As for the elect that have done good, they shall come unto me and not see death by the devouring fire. But the unrighteous the sinners, and the hypocrites shall stand in the depths of darkness that shall not pass away, and their chastisement is the fire, and angels bring forward their sins and prepare for them a place wherein they shall be punished for ever (every one according to his transgression).

Uriel (Urael) the angel of God shall bring forth the souls of those sinners (every one according to his transgression: perhaps this clause should end the preceding paragraph: so Grebaut takes it) who perished in the flood, and of all that dwelt in all idols, in every molten image, in every (object of) love, and in pictures, and of those that dwelt on all hills and in stones and by the wayside, whom men called gods: they shall burn them with them (the objects in which they dwelt, or their worshippers?) in everlasting fire; and after that all of them with their dwelling places are destroyed, they shall be punished eternally.

(Here begins the description of torments which we have, in another text, in the Akhmim fragment.)

Then shall men and women come unto the place prepared for them. By their tongues wherewith they have blasphemed the way of righteousness shall they be hanged up. There is spread under them unquenchable fire, that they escape it not.

Behold, another place: therein is a pit, great and full (of . .) In it are they that have denied righteousness: and angels of punishment chastise them and there do they kindle upon them the fire of their torment.

And again behold [two: corrupt] women: they hang them up by their neck and by their hair; they shall cast them into the pit. These are they which plaited their hair, not for good (or, not to make them beautiful) but to turn them to fornication, that they might ensnare the souls of men unto perdition. And the men that lay with them in fornication shall be hung by their loins in that place of fire; and they shall say one to another: We knew not that we should come unto everlasting punishment.

And the murderers and them that have made common cause with them shall they cast into the fire, in a place full of venomous beasts, and they shall be tormented without rest, feeling their pains; and their worms shall be as many in number as a dark cloud. And the angel Ezrael shall bring forth the souls of them that have been slain, and they shall behold the torment of them that slew them, and say one to another: Righteousness and justice is the judgement of God. For we heard, but we believed not, that we should come into this place of eternal judgement.

And near by this flame shall be a pit, great and very deep, and into it floweth from above all manner of torment, foulness, and issue. And women are swallowed up therein up to their necks and tormented with great pain. These are they that have caused their children to be born untimely, and have corrupted the work of God that created them. Over against them shall be another place where sit their children [both] alive, and they cry unto God. And flashes (lightnings) go forth from those children and pierce the eyes of them that for fornication's sake have caused their destruction.

Other men and women shall stand above them, naked; and their children stand over against them in a place of delight, and sigh and cry unto God because of their parents, saying: These are they that have despised and cursed and transgressed thy commandments and delivered us unto death: they have cursed the angel that formed us, and have hanged us up, and withheld from us (or, begrudged us) the light which thou hast given unto all creatures. And the milk of their mothers flowing from their breasts shall congeal, and from it shall come beasts devouring flesh, which shall come forth and turn and torment them for ever with their husbands, because they forsook the commandments of God and slew their children. As for their children, they shall be delivered unto the angel Temlakos (i.e. a caretaking angel: see above, in the Fragments). And they that slew them shall be tormented eternally, for God willeth it so.

Ezrael the angel of wrath shall bring men and women, the half of their bodies burning, and cast them into a place of darkness, even the hell of men; and a spirit of wrath shall chastise them with all manner of torment, and a worm that sleepeth not shall devour their entrails: and these are the persecutors and betrayers of my righteous ones.

And beside them that are there, shall be other men and women, gnawing their tongues; and they shall torment them with red-hot iron and burn their eyes. These are they that slander and doubt of my righteousness. Other men and women whose works were done in deceitfulness shall have their lips cut off, and fire entereth into their mouth and their entrails. These are the false witnesses (al. these are they that caused the martyrs to die by their lying).

And beside them, in a place near at hand, upon the stone shall be a pillar of fire, and the pillar is sharper than swords. And there shall be men and women clad in rags and filthy garments, and they shall be cast thereon, to suffer the judgement of a torment that ceaseth not: these are they that trusted in their riches and despised the widows and the woman with fatherless children . . . before God.

And into another place hard by, full of filth, do they cast men and women up to the knees. These are they that lent money and took usury.

And other men and women cast themselves down from an high place and return again and run, and devils drive them. [These are the worshippers of idols] and they put them to the end of their witst (drive them up to the top of the height) and they cast themselves down. And thus do they continually, and are tormented for ever. These are they which have cut their flesh as [apostles] of a man: and the women that were with them . . . and these are the men that defiled themselves together as women. (This is very corrupt: but the sense is clear in the (Greek.)

And beside them (shall be a brazier ?) . . . and beneath them shall the angel Ezrael prepare a place of much fire: and all the idols of gold and silver, all idols, the work of men's hands, and the semblances of images of cats and lions, of creeping things and wild beasts, and the men and women that have prepared the images thereof, shall be in chains of fire and shall be chastised because of their error before the idols, and this is their judgement for ever. (In the Greek they beat each other with rods of fire: and this is better.)

And beside them shall be other men and women, burning in the fire of the judgement, and their torment is everlasting. These are they that have forsaken the commandment of God and followed the (persuasions ?) of devils.

(Parts of these two sections are in the Bodleian Fragment. At this point the Akhmim fragment ends. The Ethiopic continues :)

And there shall be another place, very high (corrupt sentences follow. Duensing omits them: Grebaut renders doubtfully: There shall be a furnace and a brazier wherein shall burn fire. The fire that shall burn shall come from one end of the brazier). The men and women whose feet slip, shall go rolling down into a place where is fear. And again while the fire that is prepared floweth, they mount up and fall down again and continue to roll down. *(This suggests a narrow bridge over a stream of fire which they keep trying to cross.)* Thus shall they be tormented for ever. These are they that honoured not their father and mother and of their own accord withheld (withdrew) themselves from them. Therefore shall they be chastised eternally.

Furthermore the angel Ezrael shall bring children and maidens to show them those that are tormented. They shall be chastised with pains, with hanging up (?) and with a multitude of wounds which flesh-devouring birds shall inflict upon them. These are they that boast themselves (trust) in their sins, and obey not their parents and follow not the instruction of their fathers, and honour not them that are more aged than they.

Beside them shall be girls clad in darkness for a garment and they shall be sore chastised and their flesh shall be torn in pieces. These are they that kept not their virginity until they were given in marriage, and with these torments shall they be punished, and shall feel them.

And again, other men and women, gnawing their tongues without ceasing, and being tormented with everlasting fire. These are the servants (slaves) which were not obedient unto their masters; and this then is their judgement for ever.

And hard by this place of torment shall be men and women dumb and blind, whose raiment is white. They shall crowd one upon another, and fall upon coals of unquenchable fire. These are they that give alms and say: We are righteous before God: whereas they have not sought after righteousness.

Ezrael the angel of God shall bring them forth out of this fire and establish a judgement of decision. This then is their judgement. A river of fire shall flow and all judgement (they that are judged) shall be drawn down into the middle of the river. And Uriel shall set them there.

And there are wheels of fire and men and women hung thereon by the strength of the whirling thereof. And they that are in the pit shall burn: now these are the sorcerers and sorceresses. Those wheels shall be in all decision (judgement, punishment) by fire without number.

Thereafter shall the angels bring mine elect and righteous which are perfect in all uprightness, and bear them in their hands, and clothe them with the raiment of the life that is above. They shall see their desire on them that hated them, when he punisheth them, and the torment of every one shall be for ever according to his works.

And all they that are in torment shall say with one voice: have mercy upon us, for now know we the judgement of God, which he declared unto us aforetime, and we believed not. And the angel Tatirokos (Tartaruchus, keeper of hell: a word corresponding in formation to Temeluchus) shall come and chastise them with yet greater torment, and say unto them: Now do ye repent, when it is no longer the time for repentance, and nought of life remaineth. And they shall say: Righteous is the judgement of God, for we have heard and perceived that his judgement is good; for we are recompensed according to our deeds.

Then will I give unto mine elect and righteous the washing (baptism) and the salvation for which they have besought me, in the field of Akrosja (Acherousia, a lake in other writings, e.g. Apocalypse of Moses -where the soul of Adam is washed in it: see also Paul 22, 23) which is called Aneslasleja (Elysium). They shall adorn with flowers the portion of the righteous, and I shall go . . . I shall rejoice with them. I will cause the peoples to enter in to mine everlasting kingdom, and show them that eternal thing (life ?) whereon I have made them to set their hope, even I and my Father which is in heaven.

I have spoken this unto thee, Peter, and declared it unto thee. Go forth therefore and go unto the land (or city) of the west. (Duensing omits the next sentences as unintelligible; Grebaut and N. McLean render thus: and enter into the vineyard which I shall tell thee of, in order that by the sickness (sufferings) of the Son who is without sin the deeds of corruption may be sanctified. As for thee, thou art chosen according to the promise which I have given thee. Spread thou therefore my gospel throughout all the world in peace. Verily men shall rejoice: my words shall be the source of hope and of life, and suddenly shall the world be ravished.)

(We now have the section descriptive of paradise, which in the Akhmim text precedes that about hell.)

And my Lord Jesus Christ our King said unto me: Let us go unto the holy mountain. And his disciples went with him, praying. And behold there were two men there, and we could not look upon their faces, for a light came from them, shining more than the sun, and their rairment also was shining, and cannot be described, and nothing is sufficient to be compared unto them in this world. And the sweetness of them . . . that no mouth is able to utter the beauty of their appearance (or, the mouth hath not sweetness to express, &c.), for their aspect was astonishing and wonderful. And the other, great, I say (probably: and, in a word, I cannot describe it), shineth in his (sic) aspect above crystal. Like the flower of roses is the appearance of the colour of his aspect and of his body . . . his head (al. their head was a marvel). And upon his (their) shoulders (evidently something about their hair has dropped out) and on their foreheads was a crown of nard woven of fair flowers. As the rainbow in the water, [Probably: in the time of rain. From the LXX of Ezek.i.28.] so was their hair. And such was the comeliness of their countenance, adorned with all manner of ornament. And when we saw them on a sudden, we marvelled. And I drew near unto the Lord (God) Jesus Christ and said unto him: O my Lord, who are these? And he said unto me: They are Moses and Elias. And I said unto him: Abraham and Isaac and Jacob and the rest of the righteous fathers? And he showed us a great garden, open, full of fair trees and blessed fruits, and of the odour of perfumes. The fragrance thereof was pleasant and came even unto us. And thereof (al. of that tree) . . . saw I much fruit. And my Lord and God Jesus Christ said unto me: Hast thou seen the companies of the fathers?

As is their rest, such also is the honour and the glory of them that are persecuted for my righteousness' sake. And I rejoiced and believed [and believed] and understood that which is written in the book of my Lord Jesus Christ. And I said unto him: O my Lord, wilt thou that I make here three tabernacles, one for thee, and one for Moses, and one for Elias? And he said unto me in wrath: Satan maketh war against thee, and hath veiled thine understanding; and the good things of this world prevail against thee. Thine eyes therefore must be opened and thine ears unstopped that a tabernacle, not made with men's hands, which my heavenly Father hath made for me and for the elect. And we beheld it and were full of gladness.

And behold, suddenly there came a voice from heaven, saying: This is my beloved Son in whom I am well pleased: my commandments. And then came a great and exceeding white cloud over our heads and bare away our Lord and Moses and Elias. And I trembled and was afraid: and we looked up and the heaven opened and we beheld men in the flesh, and they came and greeted our Lord and Moses and Elias and went into another heaven. And the word of the scripture was fulfilled: This is the generation that seeketh him and seeketh the face of the God of Jacob. And great fear and commotion was there in heaven and the angels pressed one upon another that the word of the scripture might be fulfilled which saith: Open the gates, ye princes.

Thereafter was the heaven shut, that had been open.

And we prayed and went down from the mountain, glorifying God, which hath written the names of the righteous in heaven in the book of life.

There is a great deal more of the Ethiopic text, but it is very evidently of later date; the next words are:

'Peter opened his mouth and said to me: Hearken, my son Clement, God created all things for his glory,' and this proposition is dwelt upon. The glory of those who duly praise God is described in terms borrowed from the Apocalypse: 'The Son at his coming will raise the dead ... and will make my righteous ones shine seven times more than the sun, and will make their crowns shine like crystal and like the rainbow in the time of rain (crowns) which are perfumed with nard and cannot be contemplated (adorned) with rubies, with the colour of emeralds shining brightly, with topazes, gems, and yellow pearls that shine like the stars of heaven, and like the rays of the sun, sparkling which cannot be gazed upon.' Again, of the angels: ' Their faces shine more than the sun; their crowns are as the rainbow in the time of rain. (They are perfumed) with nard. Their eyes shine like the morning star. The beauty of their appearance cannot be expressed.... Their raiment is not woven, but white as that of the fuller, according as I saw on the mountain where Moses and Elias were. Our Lord showed at the transfiguration the apparel of the last days, of the day of resurrection, unto Peter, James and John the sons of Zebedee, and a bright cloud overshadowed us, and we heard the voice of the Father saying unto us: This is my Son whom I love and in whom I am well pleased: hear him. And being afraid we forgat all the things of this life and of the flesh, and knew not what we said because of the greatness of the wonder of that day, and of the mountain whereon he showed us the second coming in the kingdom that passeth not away.'

Next: '*The Father hath committed all judgement unto the Son.*' *The destiny of sinners -their eternal doom- is more than Peter can endure: he appeals to Christ to have pity on them.*

And my Lord answered me and said to me: 'Hast thou understood that which I said unto thee before? It is permitted unto thee to know that concerning which thou askest: but thou must not tell that which thou hearest unto the sinners lest they transgress the more, and sin.' Peter weeps many hours, and is at last consoled by an answer which, though exceedingly diffuse and vague does seem to promise ultimate pardon for all: 'My Father will give unto them all the life, the glory, and the kingdom that passeth not away,' . . . 'It is because of them that have believed in me that I am come. It is also because of them that have believed in me, that, at their word, I shall have pity on men.' The doctrine that sinners will be saved at last by the prayers of the righteous is, rather obscurely, enunciated in the Second Book of the Sibylline Oracles (a paraphrase, in this part, of the Apocalypse), and in the (Coptic) Apocalypse of Elias (see post).

Ultimately Peter orders Clement to hide this revelation in a box, that foolish men may not see it. The passage in the Second Book of the Sibylline Oracles which seems to point to the ultimate salvation of all sinners will be found in the last lines of the translation given below.

The passage in the Coptic Apocalypse of Elias is guarded and obscure in expression, but significant. It begins with a sentence which has a parallel in Peter

47

The righteous will behold the sinners in their punishment, and those who have persecuted them and delivered them up. Then will the sinners on their part behold the place of the righteous and be partakers of grace. In that day will that for which the (righteous) shall often pray, be granted to them.

That is, as I take it, the salvation of sinners will be granted at the prayer of the righteous.

Compare also the Epistle of the Apostles, 40: 'the righteous are sorry for the sinners, and pray for them.... And I will hearken unto the prayer of the righteous which they make for them.'

I would add that the author of the Acts of Paul, who (in the Third Epistle to the Corinthians and elsewhere) betrays a knowledge of the Apocalypse of Peter, makes Falconilla, the deceased daughter of Tryphaena, speak of Thecla's praying for her that she may be translated unto the place of the righteous (Thecla episode, 28).

My impression is that the maker of the Ethiopic version (or of its Arabic parent, or of another ancestor) has designedly omitted or slurred over some clauses in the passage beginning: 'Then will I give unto mine elect', and that in his very diffuse and obscure appendix to the Apocalypse, he has tried to break the dangerous doctrine of the ultimate salvation of sinners gently to his readers. But when the Arabic version of the Apocalypse is before us in the promised edition of MM. Griveau and Grebaut, we shall have better means of deciding.

APPENDIX

SECOND BOOK OF THE SIBYLLINE ORACLES, 190-338

It seems worth while to append here a translation of that portion of the Second Book which is most evidently taken from the Apocalypse of Peter. It may be remarked that Books I and II of the oracles really form but one composition, which is Christian and may be assigned to some time not early in the second century, or to the third. Many lines are borrowed from the older books, especially III and VIII.

After saying (1.187) that Elias will descend on earth and do three great signs, it proceeds:

190 Woe unto all them that are found great with child in that day, and to them that give suck to infant children, and to them that dwell by the sea (the waves). Woe to them that shall behold that day. For a dark mist shall cover the boundless world, of the east and west, the south and north. And then shall a great river of flaming fire flow from heaven and consume all places, the earth and the great ocean and the grey sea, lakes and rivers and fountains, and merciless

200 Hades and the pole of heaven: but the lights of heaven shall melt together in one and into a void (desolate) shape (?). For the stars shall all fall from heaven into the sea (?), and all souls of men shall gnash their teeth as they burn in the river of brimstone and the rush of the fire in the blazing plain, and ashes shall cover all things. And then shall all the elements of the world be laid waste, air, earth, sea, light poles, days and nights, and no more shall the multitudes of birds fly in the air nor swimming creatures any more swim the sea no ship shall sail with its cargo over the waves;

210 no straight-going oxen shall plough the tilled land; there shall be no more sound of swift winds, but he shall fuse all things together into one, and purge them clean.

214 Now when the immortal angels of the undying God Barakiel, Ramiel, Uriel, Samiel, and Azael, [These names are from Enoch.] knowing all the evil deeds that any hath wrought aforetime -then out of the misty darkness they shall bring all the souls of men to judgement, unto the seat of God the immortal, the great.

220 For he only is incorruptible, himself the Almighty, who shall be the judge of mortal men. And then unto them of the underworld shall the heavenly one give their souls and spirit and speech, and their bones joined together, with all the joints, and the flesh and sinews and veins, and skin also over the flesh, and hair as before, and the bodies of the dwellers upon earth shall be moved and arise in one day, joined together in immortal fashion and breathing.

Then shall the great angel Uriel break the monstrous bars framed of unyielding and unbroken adamant, of the brazen

230 gates of Hades, and cast them down straightway, and bring forth to judgement all the sorrowful forms, yea, of the ghosts of the ancient Titans, and of the giants, and all whom the flood overtook. And all whom the wave of the sea hath destroyed in the waters, and all whom beasts and creeping things and fowls have feasted on: all these shall he bring to the judgement seat; and again those whom flesh-devouring fire hath consumed in the flames, them also shall he gather and set before God's seat.

And when he shall overcome Fate and raise the dead, then shall Adonai Sabaoth the high thunderer sit on his heavenly

240 throne, and set up the great pillar, and Christ himself, the undying unto the undying, shall come in the clouds in glory with the pure angels, and shall sit on the seat on the right of the Great One, judging the life of the godly and the walk of ungodly men.

And Moses also the great, the friend of the Most High shall come, clad in flesh, and the great Abraham himself shall come, and Isaac and Jacob, Jesus, Daniel, Elias, Ambacum (Habakkuk), and Jonas, and they whom the Hebrews slew: and all the Hebrews that were with (after ?) Jeremias shall be judged at the judgement seat, and he shall destroy them, that they may receive a due reward and expiate all that they did in their mortal life.

And then shall all men pass through a blazing river and unquenchable flame, and the righteous shall be saved whole all of them, but the ungodly shall perish therein unto all ages, even as many as wrought evil aforetime, and committed murders, and all that were privy thereto, liars, thieves, deceivers, cruel destroyers of houses, gluttons, marriers by stealth, shedders of evil rumours, sorely insolent lawless, idolaters: and all that forsook the great immortal God and became blasphemers and harmers of the godly, breakers of faith and destroyers of righteous men. And all that look with guileful and shameless double faces -reverend priests and deacons- and judge unjustly, dealing perversely, obeying false rumours . . . more deadly than leopards and wolves, and very evil: and all that are high-minded, and usurers that heap up in their houses usury out of usury and injure orphans and widows continually: and they that give alms of unjust gain unto widows and orphans, and they that when they give alms of their own toil, reproach them; and they that have forsaken their parents in their old age and not repaid them at all, nor recompensed them for their nurture; yea, and they that have disobeyed and spoken hard words against their parents: they also that have received pledges and denied them, and servants that have turned against their masters; and again they which have defiled their flesh in lasciviousness, and have loosed the girdle of virginity in secret union, and they that make the child in the womb miscarry, and that cast out their offspring against right: sorcerers also and sorceresses with these shall the wrath of the heavenly and immortal God bring near unto the pillar, all round about which the untiring river of fire shall flow. And all of them shall the undying angels of the immortal everlasting God chastise terribly with flaming scourges, and shall bind them fast from above in fiery chains, bonds unbreakable. And then shall they cast them down in the darkness of night into Gehenna among the beasts of hell, many and frightful, where is darkness without measure.

And when they have dealt out many torments unto all whose heart was evil, thereafter out of the great river shall a wheel of fire encompass them, because they devised wicked works. And then shall they lament apart every one from another in miserable fate, fathers and infant children, mothers and sucklings weeping, nor shall they be sated with tears nor shall the voice of them that mourn piteously apart be heard (?); but far under dark and squalid Tartarus shall they cry in torment, and in no holy place shall they abide and expiate threefold every evil deed that they have done, burning in a great flame; and shall gnash their teeth, all of them worn out with fierce thirst and hunger (al. force violence), and shall call death lovely and it shall flee from them: for no more shall death nor night give them rest, and oft-times shall they beseech in vain the Almighty God, and then shall he openly turn away his face from them. For he hath granted the limit of seven ages for repentance unto men that err, by the hand of a pure virgin.

But the residue which have cared for justice and good deeds, yea, and godliness and righteous thoughts, shall angels bear up and carry through the flaming river unto light, and life without care, where is the immortal path of the great God; and three fountains, of wine and honey and milk. And the earth, common to all, not parted out with walls or fences, shall then bring forth of her own accord much fruit, and life and wealth shall be common and undistributed. For there shall be no poor man, nor rich, nor tyrant, nor slave, none great nor small any longer, no kings, no princes; but all men shall be together in common. And no more shall any man say ' night is come ', nor ' the morrow ', nor ' it was yesterday '. He maketh no more of days, nor of spring, nor winter, nor summer, nor autumn, neither marriage, nor death, nor selling, nor buying, nor set of sun, nor rising. For God shall make one long day.

And unto them, the godly, shall the almighty and immortal God grant another boon, when they shall ask it of him. He shall grant them to save men out of the fierce fire and the eternal gnashing of teeth: and this will he do, for he will gather them again out of the everlasting flame and remove them else whither, sending them for the sake of his people unto another life eternal and immortal, in the Elysian plain where are the long waves of the Acherusian lake exhaustless and deep bosomed;

Some artless iambic lines of uncertain date are appended here, which show what was thought of the doctrine:

'Plainly false: for the fire will never cease to torment the damned. I indeed could pray that it might be so, who am branded with the deepest scars of transgressions which stand in need of utmost mercy. But let Origen be ashamed of his lying words, who saith that there is a term set to the torments.'

www.ingramcontent.com/pod-product-compliance
Lightning Source LLC
LaVergne TN
LVHW041500070426
835507LV00009B/717